Travel Journal

Australia

VPJournals

Contact Details

Name:

Email address:

Tel:

Address:

Important Medical Information

Blood type:

Medication:

CONTENTS

Hi, I hope you enjoy this journal. It is packed with cool stuff and recommendations for you trip to Australia, and has plenty of space to record details of your trip.

Have fun in Australia

Great Places to visit in Australia

Bondi Beach	✓
Sydney Harbour (Sydney)	
Sydney Opera House (Sydney)	
Bondi to Coogee Beach Walk (Sydney)	
Palm Beach (Sydney)	
The Rocks (Sydney)	
Royal Botanic Gardens (Sydney)	
The Great Ocean Road (Melbourne)	
National Gallery (Melbourne)	
National Sports Museum (Melbourne)	
Melbourne Zoo (Melbourne)	
Funfields (Melbourne)	
Galactic Circus (Melbourne)	

Melbourne Cricket Ground (Melbourne)	
South Bank Parklands (Brisbane)	
Mount Coot-tha Lookout (Brisbane)	
St Helena Island (Brisbane)	
Wheel of Brisbane ferris wheel (Brisbane)	
Lone Pine Koala Sanctuary (Brisbane)	
Kings Park & Botanic Garden (Perth)	
Aviation Heritage Museum (Perth)	
Scarborough Beach (Perth)	
Penguin Island (Perth)	
Cohunu Koala Park (Perth)	
Australian War Memorial (Canberra)	
The Great Ocean Rd (Torquay)	
Mount Wellington (Hobart)	
Whitehaven Beach (Whitsunday Island)	

Cool Places to visit in Australia with Kids

Bondi Beach	✓
Sydney Harbour (Sydney)	
Sydney Opera House (Sydney)	
Bondi to Coogee Beach Walk (Sydney)	
Urban Jungle Adventure Park (Sydney)	
Palm Beach (Sydney)	
Treetop Adventure Park (Sydney)	
Bonorong Wildlife Sanctuary (Brighton)	
The Great Ocean Road (Melbourne)	
City Circle Tram (Melbourne)	
National Sports Museum (Melbourne)	
Melbourne Zoo (Melbourne)	
Funfields (Melbourne)	

Galactic Circus (Melbourne)	
Melbourne Cricket Ground (Melbourne)	
South Bank Parklands (Brisbane)	
Mount Coot-tha Lookout (Brisbane)	
St Helena Island (Brisbane)	
Wheel of Brisbane ferris wheel (Brisbane)	
Lone Pine Koala Sanctuary (Brisbane)	
Kings Park & Botanic Garden (Perth)	
Aviation Heritage Museum (Perth)	
Scarborough Beach (Perth)	
Penguin Island (Perth)	
Cohunu Koala Park (Perth)	
Australian War Memorial (Canberra)	
The Great Ocean Rd (Torquay)	
Mount Wellington (Hobart)	

Good Places to Eat in Australia

Farmhouse Kings Cross (Sydney)	✓
Twenty 8 Acres (Sydney)	
Est (Sydney)	
Bulletin Place (Sydney)	
Zahli (Sydney)	
Donna Angelina (Melbourne)	
The Colonial Tramcar (Melbourne)	
Scopri (Melbourne)	
Rice Paper Scissors (Melbourne)	
The Fat Duck (Melbourne)	
Black Hide Steakhouse (Brisbane)	
Sono (Brisbane)	

1889 Enoteca (Brisbane)	
La Vue Waterfront (Brisbane)	
Miel Container (Brisbane)	
D's Authentic Japanese (Perth)	
Nunzio's (Perth)	
Juniper & Bay (Perth)	
Friends Restaurant (Perth)	
Maruzzella (Perth)	
Courgette (Canberra)	
Pomegranate (Canberra)	
Olive at Mawson (Canberra)	
Black Fire (Canberra)	
Aubergine (Canberra)	

Best Websites to Research Further

Do some more research on the internet to plan your trip:

www.Australia.com
www.familydaysout.com/australia/
www.Sydney.com
www.VisitMelbourne.com
www.VisitBrisbane.com.au
www.PerthTouristCentre.com.au
www.VisitCanberra.com.au
www.wikipedia.org/wiki/Australia
www.nomadicmatt.com/travel-guides/Australia-travel-tips/

More places I want to visit on our trip

1. _____

2. _____

3. _____

4. _____

5. _____

6. _____

7. _____

8. _____

9. _____

10. _____

11. _____

12. _____

13. _____

14. _____

15. _____

Postcard List

Name:
Address:

Name:
Address:

Name:
Address:

Name:

Address:

Name:

Address:

Name:

Address:

Name:

Address:

Name:

Address:

Name:

Address:

Name:

Address:

Name:

Address:

Name:

Address:

Name:

Address:

Name:

Address:

MAIL

Packing List

✔	This Journal
	Tickets
	Passport
	Money
	Chargers
	Batteries
	Book to read
	Camera
	Tablet
	Sun glasses
	Sun cream

	Toiletries
	Water
	Watch
	Snacks
	Umbrella
	Towel
	Guide book
	Kindle
	Jacket
	Medication
	Add more below

Australia Facts

- Australia is the 6th largest country in the world, occupying 7.6 million square kilometres. There are approximately 22 million people living in Australia

- The largest cities in Australia are Sydney, Melbourne, Brisbane, Perth and Adelaide

- Vegetation covers nearly 7 million square kilometres or 91 percent of Australia

- The largest Greek population in the world beside Athens in Greece can be found in Melbourne Victoria.

- Australia hosted the 1956 (Melbourne) and 2000 (Sydney) Summer Olympics

- Australia is home to a variety of unique animals, including the koala, kangaroo, emu, kookaburra and platypus

- It is estimated that humans have lived in Australia for around 45,000 years

- The name 'Australia' comes from the Latin word 'australis', meaning southern

- The world's largest reef system, the Great Barrier Reef, is found off the north-eastern coast of Australia

- It has 16 world heritage listed sites including historic townships, cities and landscapes

- Australia was the second country in the world to give women the right to vote in 1902

- Australians refer to English people as Pome, which is actually the acronym for Prisoners of Mother England

- Approximately 1.35 trillion bottles of wine are produced by Australia

Clothes & Shoe Sizes

Children's Shoe Sizes

UK	EUROPE	US	Japan
4	20	4½ or 5	12 ½
4 ½	21	5 or 5½	13
5	21 or 22	5½ or 6	13 ½
5 ½	22	6	13½ or 14
6	23	6½ or 7	14 or 14½
6 ½	23 or 24	7 ½	14½ or 15
7	24	7½ or 8	15
7 ½	25	8 or 9	15 ½
8	25 or 26	8½ or 9	16
8 ½	26	9½	16 ½
9	27	9½ or 10	16 ½ or 17
10	28	10½ or 11	17 ½
10½ or 11	29	11½ or 12	18
11 ½	30	12½	18 or 18 ½
12	31	13	19 or 19 ½
12 ½	31	13 or 13½	19 ½ or 20
13	32	1	20
13 ½	32 ½	1 ½	20 ½
1	33	1½ or 2	21
2	34	2½ or 3	22

Children's Clothing Sizes

UK	EUROPE	US	Australia
12m	80cm	12-18m	12m
18m	80-86cm	18-24m	18m
24m	86-92cm	23-24m	2
2-3	92-98cm	2T	3
3-4	98-104cm	4T	4
3-5	104-110cm	5	5
5-6	110-116cm	6	6
6-7	116-122cm	6X-7	7
7-8	122-128cm	7 to 8	8
8-9	128-134cm	9 to 10	9
9-10	134-140cm	10	10
10-11	140-146cm	11	11
11-12	146-152cm	14	12

Women's Shoe Sizes

UK	EUROPE	US	Japan
3	35 ½	5	22 ½
3 ½	36	5 ½	23
4	37	6	23
4 ½	37 ½	6 ½	23 ½
5	38	7	24
5 ½	39	7 ½	24
6	39 ½	8	24 ½
6 ½	40	8 ½	25
7	41	9 ½	25 ½
7 ½	41 ½	10	26
8	42	10 ½	26 ½

Women's Clothes Sizes

UK	US	Japan	France / Spain	Germany	Australia	Australia
6/8	6	7-9	36	34	40	8
10	8	9-11	38	36	42	10
12	10	11-13	40	38	44	12
14	12	13-15	42	39	46	14
16	14	15-17	44	40	48	16
18	16	17-19	46	42	50	18
20	18	19-21	48	44	52	20

Men's Shoe Sizes

UK	EUROPE	US	Japan
6	38 ½	6 ½	24 ½
6 ½	39	7	25
7	40	7 ½	25 ½
7 ½	41	8	26
8	42	8 ½	27 ½
8 ½	43	9	27 ½
9	43 ½	9 ½	28
9 ½	44	10	28 ½
10	44	10 ½	28 ½
10 ½	44 ½	11	29
11	45	12	29 ½

Men's Suit / Coat / Sweater Sizes

UK / US / Aus	EU / Japan	General
32	42	Small
34	44	Small
36	46	Small
38	48	Medium
40	50	Large
42	52	Large
44	54	Extra Large
46	56	Extra Large

Men's Pants / Trouser Sizes (Waist)

UK / US	Europe
32	81 cm
34	86 cm
36	91 cm
38	97 cm
40	102 cm
42	107 cm

We have included another copy of this at the back of the book, so you can find it quickly again when you are in Australia

Australia Trip Diary

Write a daily diary during your trip

Day 1

Date: _____   **Weather:** _____

_____

_____

_____

_____

_____

_____

_____

_____

_____

_____

_____

_____

_____

_____

Day 2

Date: _____   **Weather:** _____

_____

_____

_____

_____

_____

_____

_____

_____

_____

_____

_____

_____

_____

_____

_____

Day 3

Date: _____   **Weather:** _____

_____

_____

_____

_____

_____

_____

_____

_____

_____

_____

_____

_____

_____

_____

_____

_____

Day 4

Date: _____   **Weather:** _____

_____

_____

_____

_____

_____

_____

_____

_____

_____

_____

_____

_____

_____

_____

Day 5

Date: _____   Weather: _____

_____

_____

_____

_____

_____

_____

_____

_____

_____

_____

_____

_____

_____

_____

Day 6

Date: _____   Weather: _____

_____

_____

_____

_____

_____

_____

_____

_____

_____

_____

_____

_____

_____

Day 7

Date: _____   **Weather:** _____

_____

_____

_____

_____

_____

_____

_____

_____

_____

_____

_____

_____

_____

_____

Day 8

Date: _____   Weather: _____

_____

_____

_____

_____

_____

_____

_____

_____

_____

_____

_____

_____

_____

_____

Day 9

Date: _____   **Weather:** _____

_____

_____

_____

_____

_____

_____

_____

_____

_____

_____

_____

_____

_____

Day 10

Date: _____   **Weather:** _____

_____

_____

_____

_____

_____

_____

_____

_____

_____

_____

_____

_____

Day 11

Date: _____   Weather: _____

_____

_____

_____

_____

_____

_____

_____

_____

_____

_____

_____

_____

_____

_____

Day 12

Date: _____   Weather: _____

_____

_____

_____

_____

_____

_____

_____

_____

_____

_____

_____

_____

_____

Day 13

Date: _____   Weather: _____

_____

_____

_____

_____

_____

_____

_____

_____

_____

_____

_____

_____

_____

_____

_____

Day 14

Date: _____   **Weather:** _____

_____

_____

_____

_____

_____

_____

_____

_____

_____

_____

_____

_____

_____

_____

Day 15

Date: _____   Weather: _____

_____

_____

_____

_____

_____

_____

_____

_____

_____

_____

_____

_____

_____

_____

Day 16

Date: _____   Weather: _____

_____

_____

_____

_____

_____

_____

_____

_____

_____

_____

_____

_____

_____

Day 17

Date: _____   **Weather:** _____

_____

_____

_____

_____

_____

_____

_____

_____

_____

_____

_____

_____

_____

_____

Day 18

Date: _____   Weather: _____

_____

_____

_____

_____

_____

_____

_____

_____

_____

_____

_____

_____

_____

Day 19

Date: _____   **Weather:** _____

_____

_____

_____

_____

_____

_____

_____

_____

_____

_____

_____

_____

_____

_____

_____

Day 20

Date: _____   Weather: _____

_____

_____

_____

_____

_____

_____

_____

_____

_____

_____

_____

_____

_____

_____

Day 21

Date: _____   Weather: _____

_____

_____

_____

_____

_____

_____

_____

_____

_____

_____

_____

_____

_____

_____

Memories of your Trip

Things I will remember from the trip

Favorite Places visited on the Trip

People I Met

Name:
Address:
Tel:
email:

Name:
Address:
Tel:
email:

Name:
Address:
Tel:
email:

Name:
Address:
Tel:
email:

Name:
Address:
Tel:
email:

Name:
Address:
Tel:
email:

Name:
Address:
Tel:
email:

Name:
Address:
Tel:
email:

Name:
Address:
Tel:
email:

Name:
Address:
Tel:
email:

Name:
Address:
Tel:
email:

We hope you enjoyed your trip to Australia

Please leave us a review if you found this Journal useful

Check out our useful resources on the next few pages

Clothes & Shoe Sizes

Children's Shoe Sizes

UK	EUROPE	US	Japan
4	20	4½ or 5	12 ½
4 ½	21	5 or 5½	13
5	21 or 22	5½ or 6	13 ½
5 ½	22	6	13½ or 14
6	23	6½ or 7	14 or 14½
6 ½	23 or 24	7 ½	14½ or 15
7	24	7½ or 8	15
7 ½	25	8 or 9	15 ½
8	25 or 26	8½ or 9	16
8 ½	26	9½	16 ½
9	27	9½ or 10	16 ½ or 17
10	28	10½ or 11	17 ½
10½ or 11	29	11½ or 12	18
11 ½	30	12½	18 or 18 ½
12	31	13	19 or 19 ½
12 ½	31	13 or 13½	19 ½ or 20
13	32	1	20
13 ½	32 ½	1 ½	20 ½
1	33	1½ or 2	21
2	34	2½ or 3	22

Children's Clothing Sizes

UK	EUROPE	US	Australia
12m	80cm	12-18m	12m
18m	80-86cm	18-24m	18m
24m	86-92cm	23-24m	2
2-3	92-98cm	2T	3
3-4	98-104cm	4T	4
3-5	104-110cm	5	5
5-6	110-116cm	6	6
6-7	116-122cm	6X-7	7
7-8	122-128cm	7 to 8	8
8-9	128-134cm	9 to 10	9
9-10	134-140cm	10	10
10-11	140-146cm	11	11
11-12	146-152cm	14	12

Women's Shoe Sizes

UK	EUROPE	US	Japan
3	35 ½	5	22 ½
3 ½	36	5 ½	23
4	37	6	23
4 ½	37 ½	6 ½	23 ½
5	38	7	24
5 ½	39	7 ½	24
6	39 ½	8	24 ½
6 ½	40	8 ½	25
7	41	9 ½	25 ½
7 ½	41 ½	10	26
8	42	10 ½	26 ½

Women's Clothes Sizes

UK	US	Japan	France / Spain	Germany	Australia	Australia
6/8	6	7-9	36	34	40	8
10	8	9-11	38	36	42	10
12	10	11-13	40	38	44	12
14	12	13-15	42	39	46	14
16	14	15-17	44	40	48	16
18	16	17-19	46	42	50	18
20	18	19-21	48	44	52	20

Men's Shoe Sizes

UK	EUROPE	US	Japan
6	38 ½	6 ½	24 ½
6 ½	39	7	25
7	40	7 ½	25 ½
7 ½	41	8	26
8	42	8 ½	27 ½
8 ½	43	9	27 ½
9	43 ½	9 ½	28
9 ½	44	10	28 ½
10	44	10 ½	28 ½
10 ½	44 ½	11	29
11	45	12	29 ½

Men's Suit / Coat / Sweater Sizes

UK / US / Aus	EU / Japan	General
32	42	Small
34	44	Small
36	46	Small
38	48	Medium
40	50	Large
42	52	Large
44	54	Extra Large
46	56	Extra Large

Men's Pants / Trouser Sizes (Waist)

UK / US	Europe
32	81 cm
34	86 cm
36	91 cm
38	97 cm
40	102 cm
42	107 cm

Common Translations

English	French	Spanish	Italian
Hello	Bonjour	Hola	Ciao
Goodbye	Au revoir	Adiós	Arrivederci
Yes	Oui	Sí	Si
No	Non	No	No
Please	S'il-vous-plaît	Por favor	Per favore
Thank you	Merci	Gracias	Grazie
Excuse me	Excusez-moi	Perdón	Mi scusi
How much	Combien	Cuánto	Quanto
My name is	Mon nom est	Mi nombre es	Io mi chiamo
Where is	Où est	Dónde está	Dov'è
The bank	La banque	El banco	La banca
The toilet	Les toilettes	El baño	Il bagno

German	Japanese	Mandarin	Hindi
Hallo	Kon'nichiwa	Ni hao	Namaste
Auf Wiedersehen	Sayonara	Zaijian	Alavida
Ja	Hai	Shi de	Ham
Nein	Ie	Meiyou	Nahim
Bitte	Onegaishimasu	Qing	Krpaya
Vielen Dank	Arigato	Xiexie	Dhan'yavada
Entschuldigung	Sumimasen	Duoshao	Mujhe mapha karem
Wie viel	Ikura	Wo de mingzi shi	Kitana
Mein Name ist	Watashinonamaeha	Nali	Mera nama hai
Wo ist	Doko ni aru	Yinhang	Kaham hai
Die Bank	Ginko	Yinhang	Bainka
Die Toilette	Toire	Cesuo	Saucalaya

Notes:

Made in the USA
Coppell, TX
20 February 2023

13089668R00077